I0012137

Garbage Collection
Algorithms
Optimizing Memory Management

Table of Contents

Chapter 1. Introduction

In the dawn of the Information Age, it's easy to overlook the hum of constant activity beneath the sleek surface of our digital devices — an extensive, sophisticated choreography ensuring optimum performance. However, at the heart of these complex systems, there's an unsung hero we sometimes take for granted — the Garbage Collection Algorithm. In our Special Report, "Garbage Collection Algorithms: Optimizing Memory Management," we delve into the multidimensional labyrinth of this crucial component in the design and operation of our needy computational systems. Don't let the jargon deter you; we've gone to extensive lengths to demystify this subject, narrating it in a captivatingly down-to-earth approach. Success in the digital realm is stitched into the fabric of understanding its basic tools, and there's nothing basic about garbage collection algorithms—they run the show. Join us as we explore this intricate intersection where computer science, logic, and performance optimization meet.

Chapter 2. Unveiling Memory Management: The Basics

Before we can discuss the importance and intricacies of garbage collection algorithms, it is critical to understand the realm they inhabit—the domain of memory management. This critical aspect of computing ensures that systems store, access, and manipulate data efficiently, making memory management the backbone of successful computational operations.

2.1. Understanding Memory

At its most basic, computer memory is a finite resource—a playground where computational actions happen. This playground can be uneven, with different areas that offer distinct capabilities and characteristics. These areas include the stack, the heap, and registers that play different roles in the functioning of the computer.

Stack memory is used for static memory allocation, where the size and lifetime of variables are known at compile time. It's organized, predictable, and addresses the space consumed by a program in a manner akin to neatly arranged books on a shelf. Memory allocated on the Stack is managed for you by the compiler and is automatically cleaned up when the scope that it was declared in is no longer in use.

Heap memory, on the other hand, is used for dynamic memory allocation where the size or the lifetime of the used memory cannot be predicted at compile time. Unlike a stack, it is like an untidy room, where blocks of memory are allocated and cleaned up in potentially unpredictable patterns, giving the heap its often fragmented nature.

Computers also store critical data in registers, embedded directly within the CPU, and offer the highest speed of data access for the most immediately essential information.

2.2. Memory Management Goals

Effective memory management serves three basic goals:

- Efficient use of memory: The algorithm must provide high throughput by maximizing the number of processes in the memory, thereby reducing retrieval time from secondary storage.

- Fair allocation of memory: The algorithm must distribute memory equitably among processes such that each process is allocated as much memory as it requires, but not more than it needs.

- Enabling sharing and protection: The algorithm must manage the memory in such a way that processes can share memory areas without corrupting one another's data.

2.3. The Lifecycle of Memory

Understanding the lifecycle of memory is crucial. The lifecycle has four stages: allocation, use, deallocation, and recycling. In the allocation stage, the system assigns a block of memory based on the requirements of a process. During the use stage, the process accesses and modifies this memory. In the deallocation stage, the process is finished with the memory, signaled by explicitly freeing it or exiting. Finally, in the recycling stage, the deallocated memory space is given back to the system, to be allocated again in the future.

2.4. Memory Leaks and Dangling Pointers

Correct memory management requires handling a couple of infamous issues - memory leaks and dangling pointers.

A memory leak happens when memory has been allocated, used, but not deallocated suitably, thus making it unavailable for later use. Repeatedly leaking memory can lead to a system gradually slowing down or even crashing when it runs out of memory.

A dangling pointer occurs when a piece of memory is deallocated while pointers are still referring to it. Attempts to use such pointers can lead to unpredictable and possibly catastrophic behavior since the memory could be reassigned and modified.

2.5. Automatic Memory Management

The process of managing memory isn't always a manual, developer-guided one. Higher-level languages like Python, Java, and JavaScript come with automated memory management, reducing the chances of memory leaks or dangling pointers.

These systems use a technique known as Garbage Collection (GC), where the system keeps track of memory that's in use and memory that's no longer being used by any part of the program. The GC then automatically deallocates—or "collects"—the garbage, freeing up memory for future use.

This fundamental understanding of memory and the necessity of its proper management paves the way for the discussion of how garbage collection algorithms function. As we proceed, we will look into multiple garbage collection algorithms, their operations, and their implications on the performance of your applications and systems.

So buckle up as we prepare to dive into the heart of memory management—a journey into the realm of garbage collection algorithms.

Chapter 3. The Life Cycle of Data: From Creation to Deletion

Let's start our discourse by examining the life cycle of data within a computer system. It's quite similar to a living organism. It's born, it lives, and eventually, it dies. But what sets the life of data apart is the delicate and intricate process that goes into managing its lifespan—an endeavor handled predominantly by the unsung hero of our digital world, the Garbage Collection Algorithm.

The stages that a piece of data undergoes from the time it is created to when it is deleted are critical to understanding how our digital devices operate. Let's look at each step in detail.

3.1. Creation of Data

To comprehend how data is deleted, we must first grasp how it is created. Every time you run a program or command, your device spawns data. Even as you read this line, your device is generating it. It's just how the digital landscape works.

If you initiate a command or a procedure in an application, data in the form of objects or variables is produced. The data birthed isn't merely raw, unstructured information. It's structured and tailored to conform to the requirements of the specific program in which it was produced. This ensures the overall efficiency of the system, as structured data is simpler to manage and process.

3.2. Allocation of Memory

As soon as the data is generated, it must find a home—a foundation of memory where it is stored and able to perform its intended tasks. This step is known as memory allocation and involves placing the data into memory locations. But it's not a casual, arbitrary process. Rather, it's a meticulous choreography designed to ensure optimal utilization of memory resources.

There are mainly two types of memory allocations—stack and heap. Stack memory is characterized by its sequential and deterministic manner. It's often used for static data whose size and lifespan are known and predictable.

On the other hand, heap memory is dynamic and can expand and contract based on the data's needs. This flexibility allows it to handle dynamic data—the kind whose size and lifespan are unpredictable and can alter as per the program's requirements.

3.3. Living the Data Life

Once securely homed in memory, the data lives its life. This phase of the life cycle is when the magic happens—the data does what it was born to do. It's used and manipulated, ushering in results, solutions, operations, and a whole lot more. Every click you resolve, video you stream, or calculation you execute involves data living its life.

During this phase, data may be modified, moved, read, and processed in countless ways depending on user interactions and programmatic needs. It may spawn more data, get bundled with other data or be segmented into smaller pieces—its "lifestyle" molded by the requirements of the programs it serves.

3.4. Deterioration and the Need for Disposal

As with all things, data too cannot live forever. There comes a point when it has served its purpose and is no longer needed. Unchecked and unexpurgated, such obsolete data, often termed as garbage, consumes valuable resources. The toxic effects of accumulated garbage are impeded system performance and, in severe cases, potential system failures.

Therefore, the need to dispose of data arises—the need for a system to identify data that is no longer needed and eradicate it. It's the culmination of a data's life cycle, akin to a digital version of the circle of life.

3.5. Garbage Collection

Here enters the hero of our story—the garbage collector. It's a memory management technique designed to automate the process of identifying and eliminating garbage—effectively recycling memory that was previously occupied by now-defunct data.

Garbage collectors vary in complexity and strategy, ranging from simple reference counting collectors to intricate, phase-based, concurrent collectors. Regardless of the implementational details, their purpose is to ensure optimum utilization of memory resources, thereby smoothing the way for a system's ceaseless, efficient operation.

3.6. Finishing Touches

With the garbage cleared, the reclaimed memory is now available to house newborn data, and the cycle begins anew. The intricate ballet that is data life cycle management continues unabated, carefully controlled by the garbage collection algorithms.

As we've seen, the life cycle of data is not a simple journey from creation to deletion. Instead, it's a complex process involving several stages, each of which plays a crucial role in ensuring the smooth running of our digital devices. However, the role of garbage collection—while mostly invisible—is particularly noteworthy, pivotal as it is in keeping our systems efficient and maintaining the careful balance that allows the seamless interplay of creation and deletion to continue.

Chapter 4. Garbage Collection: A Dark Horse in Computing?

If the heart of your machine was an orchestra, consider the garbage collection algorithm as the conductor. It orchestrates when resources are used and when retired, maintaining an effective and efficient system. But, what is this elusive choreographer of computational efficiency?

4.1. What is Garbage Collection?

Garbage Collection (GC) or automatic memory management, is a critical process within the runtime execution model of several programming languages such as Java, Python, .NET, and more. This process is responsible for allocating and deallocating memory automatically so developers can focus on core application logic rather than getting entangled in the fine details of memory management.

4.2. Historical Overview

The concept of garbage collection originated in the 1950s and 60s, when manual memory management was a complex endeavor and prone to issues such as memory leaks and damage. It was first conceptualised by John McCarthy while developing Lisp, one of the early high-level programming languages. Since then, the need for efficient memory management has burgeoned with more complex applications' evolution, and garbage collection has grown accordingly.

4.3. Why Does Garbage Collection Matter?

GC plays a critical role in enhancing software and system reliability. It reconciles the disparity between the physical memory space's limited size and the abstraction of infinity granted by the virtual memory space. This whole process pays significant dividends; more available memory can be accessed faster, easing the execution of larger, more memory-intensive applications.

The garbage collection process prevents memory leaks (where memory chosen by a program is not released back) and dangling pointers (a reference to a memory address that has already been freed). Thus, avoiding system slowdowns or crashes due to out of memory (OOM) situations.

4.4. The Process of Garbage Collection

The GC process involves two key steps: identifying when a piece of data is no longer needed and reclaiming the memory resources that the unwanted data once occupied.

On a high level, garbage collection consists of three operations: marking, sweeping, and compacting.

1. Marking: The GC algorithm traverses the application and marks each object it can reach as live. Any object not marked is considered garbage since the application can no longer access it.

2. Sweeping: Next, the GC sweeps through the memory to remove the 'garbage'--the objects not marked as live.

3. Compacting: Finally, the GC relocates the live objects to one part of the memory area, making it easier to allocate new objects

adjacent to existing ones.

4.5. Garbage Collection Algorithms

There are several approaches to doing garbage collection, each with its unique strengths and weaknesses.

1. Reference Counting: This technique counts how many references point to a particular object. If a block has zero references, it is garbage collected. This method is simple and straightforward but fails in cases of circular references.

2. Mark and Sweep: This algorithm marks all accessible objects, then sweeps through and frees all unmarked (or 'dead') objects. It takes a lot of time and processing power and can cause program execution suspension.

3. Stop and Copy: This is a two-space garbage collection algorithm. The total available memory gets divided into two halves. Upon collection, it starts from the root, copying all live objects to the other half of the memory space, and then swaps the spaces. The old half gets cleared completely. This method is quick but consumes much memory.

4. Generational GC: This technique divides the heap into a few generations (young, old, and permanent). Most new objects are dead quickly, so it performs GC on younger generations more frequently, significantly improving GC performance.

4.6. Balancing Performance and Garbage Collection

Tuning a garbage collection algorithm is crucial for a system's performance. Long pauses due to GC may interrupt program execution and lead to slow system responses, known as 'GC pauses.' Hence, optimizing GC has always been a significant challenge.

The tuning process depends on many factors, like the choice of programming language, the nature of the application, the specific GC algorithm used, machine architecture, and more. It's important to regularly monitor and tune the GC according to the changing load and usage conditions of the application.

4.7. Conclusion

The garbage collection algorithm is undoubtedly one of the most important utilities underpinning the smooth operation of high-level languages. Its evolution and continued development are pivotal for the forward march of the Information Age. As systems grow more complex and robust, GC algorithms will continue taking the strain of memory management, increasingly improving our systems' efficiency and reliability. It may always remain the 'dark horse' in computing - unseen, unsung, yet unequivocally essential.

Chapter 5. From Iterative to Generational: Types of Garbage Collection Algorithms

Computational systems rely extensively on resource management, particularly memory management, to perform in an optimal manner. A significant aspect of this involves gathering and disposing of "garbage," or unused data in memory. Over the years, multiple algorithms have been employed to handle this task, each with its own advantages, disadvantages, and suitable use contexts. Broadly, these systems can be divided into two categories - iterative and generational garbage collection algorithms.

5.1. An Overview of Iterative Garbage Collection

Iterative garbage collection works on the premise that "what is not used must be freed." It primarily uses two techniques - reference counting and tracing (also known as mark and sweep).

Reference counting works by keeping a count of how many variables refer to an object. Once an object is no longer being referred to (i.e., its reference count is zero), it is understood to be "garbage" and can thus be disposed of. Despite its simplicity and predictability, reference counting falls short in identifying cyclic references, situations where a group of objects refers to each other but not to any external object.

In response to this setback, the tracing approach was developed. The tracing garbage collection algorithm, also known as the mark-and-sweep algorithm, works by "marking" objects that are reachable from the root (or from global variables). After a full traversal (mark phase), the algorithm "sweeps" through memory, freeing up space taken by unmarked objects (sweep phase).

While the tracing approach, in general, is more efficient and solves the cyclic reference problem, it pays for this benefit at the cost of periodic pauses. During the mark-and-sweep phase, the program must be paused. These pauses, also known as "stop the world" events, can affect the smooth running of the application, especially in a real-time system.

5.2. Transition to Generational Garbage Collection

The algorithmic inefficiencies of the iterative garbage collection approach led to the innovation of the generational garbage collection algorithm. Generational garbage collection capitalizes on two key observations within many computational systems:

1. Most objects die young: This is often referred to as the "infant mortality" or "generational hypothesis." It states that if an object survives its infant stage, it is likely to be long-lived. This has been found to hold true for many programming languages, including Java, Python, and Ruby.

2. Inter-generational pointers are rare: Not many older objects point to newer objects.

This design of the generational garbage collector takes advantage of the above observations to massage the stop-the-world problem and optimize the time-cost ratio inherent in garbage collection. It does this by dividing the heap memory into generations (usually two): the young generation and the old generation.

New objects are placed into the young generation, which is composed of the Eden space—where new objects are initially allocated— and two Survivor spaces. When the Eden space fills up, a minor garbage collection is triggered. It doesn't clean the entire heap; rather, it only cleans the young generation, thus increasing the efficiency and reducing the "stop the world" duration. Objects that survive several minor garbage collections, are moved to the old generation.

The old generation is collected less frequently and, as it is the location of longer-lived objects, contains less "garbage". Its infrequent "stop the world" events are known as major collections and are more costly.

It is in striking this balance, that the generational garbage collection algorithm optimizes memory management more efficiently than its iterative counterparts, resulting in better application performance.

5.3. Subtle Flavors: Variations of the Generational Technique

Just as there were variations in the iterative garbage collection strategy, multiple flavors of the generational strategy have also been developed, with each offering its own unique benefits, and suited for different computing scenarios. Key amongst these variations are three: the concurrent mark-sweep (CMS) collector, the parallel collector, and the most recent G1 collector.

The CMS collector was designed to address the long pause times of the major garbage collections in old generations. Its strategy involves allowing both the garbage collector and the application to concurrently run by breaking the collection process into incremental parts. In this manner, it aims to offer a smoother user experience, especially in interactive applications.

Next is the parallel collector, also known as the throughput collector. While it sacrifices short pause times, it compensates for this with better overall throughput. It does this by using multiple threads to execute the major collections, thus reducing total garbage collection time. This is especially suitable for batch processing tasks and applications where maximum throughput is desired.

Finally, the G1 collector, or Garbage-First collector, is an attempt to combine the strengths of the previous approaches. It aims to offer more predictable pause times while also maintaining high throughput. The G1 collector achieves this by dividing the heap into many small regions and prioritizing the collection of the regions with the most garbage, thus the name "Garbage-First."

5.4. Fine-tuning garbage collection: A balancing act

Regardless of the garbage collection strategy adopted, it is paramount to understand that garbage collection tuning is a delicate act of balancing memory use, throughput, and pause times. As such, careful adjustments, continuous monitoring, and an understanding of the specifics of these algorithms are critical to ensure optimal operation, especially in systems where any aspect of performance is sensitive.

Garbage collection is a lively, evolving field that continues to shape the backbone of our computational systems. As computing systems become more complex and demanding, the need for efficient resource management only grows. Understanding the types of garbage collection algorithms—from the iterative reference counting and tracing algorithms to the generational variants—is the first step towards optimizing and managing these systems effectively.

Chapter 6. Uninhibited Power: Automatic Memory Management

In any information processing system, be it your trusted smartphone or the massive data center running your favorite online service, memory management is of the essence. At the heart of memory management is a process known as garbage collection (GC). GC is tasked with identifying and freeing up computer memory that is no longer in use by a program. As we proceed, you'll find the discussion will pull from various corners of computer science, including programming languages, algorithms, and data structures.

6.1. The Foundations

At its core, a GC algorithm answers two primary questions: When should the garbage collection process take place? And, exactly which segments of memory should this process consider freeing? The answers to these questions rely on concepts such as understanding reachability and automatic memory management.

In layman's terms, we consider a chunk of memory to be "reachable" if there's a reference to it somewhere in the live data of the program (variables, objects) that can trace back a path to a root or a set of roots (roots are often global variables and active threads). If a piece of data is 'not reachable,' it is essentially considered 'dead' or 'garbage,' and thus, it's memory ripe for reclaiming.

Automatic memory management, as an overarching concept, includes garbage collection as well as processes like memory allocation. The essence is that the responsibility of memory management is shifted from the developer to the runtime environment. This helps eliminate common issues such as memory leaks (when program keeps holding onto memory and doesn't release it back to the system even after it's clearly done with it).

6.2. Algorithms of Choice

There's a variety of GC algorithms, each with its mechanism of operation, pros, and cons. An example of a four-stage algorithm—Mark-Sweep-Compact—is as follows:

- Mark: In this phase, the GC identifies which pieces of memory are still in use by marking the reachable objects.

- Sweep: Here, the GC sweeps through the heap memory, freeing the memory blocks of unmarked objects.

- Compact: To mitigate fragmentation—when memory is broken up into pieces—the GC moves all marked objects, so they are contiguous.

- Update: The GC updates the references to these objects to their new locations.

Another is the Reference Counting Algorithm, which keeps a count of the number of references to each object in the memory. An object's memory is freed when its reference count hits zero.

6.3. Adjusting for Performance

On the surface, it looks like we should have our GC execute as often as possible to keep memory as available as possible. However, remember that garbage collection itself requires computational resources. It's a classic case of trade-offs — more aggressive garbage collection can cause slower overall program execution.

Different applications have different needs: real-time systems might need a consistently fast response time; data centers might be more concerned about maximizing throughput. Thus, the choice of when and how aggressive the GC algorithm should function is starkly dependent on the use-case.

6.4. Communication with Memory

The manner in which the GC interacts with memory and how effectively it handles this crucial resource has a significant impact on the overall performance of the system. There are various forms of memory that a GC has to work with, such as Heap memory, Stack memory, and PermGen (Permanent Generation) memory. Each of these has their own nuances, and managing them effectively can bring significant efficiency to the entire system.

6.5. Tuning the Garbage Collector

A GC is not a one-size-fits-all solution. Developers and system administrators often have to fine-tune the garbage collector according to the application's need. This can involve adjusting thresholds, tuning specific algorithms, and picking the right 'stop-the-world' moments when the GC can perform its clean-up.

6.6. The Future of Garbage Collection

With the ever-growing needs of today's applications and the surge in distributed computing, GC algorithms need to adapt. Future GCs are projected to be increasingly concurrent, pauseless, and better integrated with the application's operation to ensure smooth performance.

What lies beneath the surface of our technological marvels is an intricate dance of logic, performance optimization, and memory management. In this dance, the garbage collector serves as a conductor, ensuring the seamless performance of our computational systems. Stay tuned for our next chapter where we dive deep into specific garbage collection algorithms and uncover their underlying principles.

Chapter 7. Stop-The-World Vs. Concurrent: A Comparative Analysis

The world of garbage collection algorithms (GCAs) is abundant with variants, but two principle types come to prominence: 'Stop-The-World' (STW) and 'Concurrent'. It's essential to note, before plunging into the comparative analysis, that both types carry their own perks and drawbacks depending on the system requirements and execution environment.

7.1. Defining Stop-The-World (STW)

Let's begin with STW. This garbace collection process pauses (stops) the application entirely throughout the operation. Consequently, all processing time is dedicated to identifying and removing unused objects in the memory—thus the term 'Stop-The-World'. While it might sound drastic to halt everything completely, STW's advantages come in its simplicity and its comprehensive cleaning approach.

1. *Efficiency*: STW approach ensures thorough cleaning which, in turn, paves the way for efficient memory allocation for forthcoming tasks.

2. *Predictability*: Since all application tasks are halted during the operations, STW GCAs result in predictable memory usage patterns.

However, a glaring downside of STW is the risk of application freezing, especially in systems demanding low-latency responses.

7.2. Defining Concurrent GC

Parallel to STW, we have Concurrent garbage collection. Unlike STW, Concurrent GC operates simultaneously with the execution of the application—thus the name 'Concurrent'. By performing garbage collection in real-time alongside the tasks, one could anticipate a reduced impact on the system's responsiveness. Here are the noteworthy benefits:

1. *User Experience*: No application-stop means no apparent delay to the end-user, leading to improved user experience, especially in interactive applications.

2. *Real-time Processing*: Concurrent GC is advantageous for real-time systems as it ensures continuous processing.

Yet, the Concurrent approach isn't devoid of shortcomings. Namely, these algorithms generally require more CPU resources and might complicate the object's lifecycle due to their simultaneous nature. Plus, there's a risk of race conditions and inconsistencies that may arise due to the algorithm running concurrently with the application.

7.3. The Abridged Comparative Analysis

Moving on from a basic definition, let's juxtapose the two in a comparative analysis with regards to a few common parameters.

7.4. Performance

STW shines in systems where thorough memory cleaning surpasses real-time performance needs, e.g., in batch-processing systems. On the contrary, Concurrent is the go-to for systems focusing on latency-sensitive applications or interactive platforms where response times are crucial.

7.5. Complexity

The STW approach proves less complicated due to the absence of concurrency. Working sequentially, one task at a time, it's straightforward, providing predictable outcomes, and easy to implement. Contrariwise, concurrent GCs need to tackle the complexities of running simultaneously with application execution—increasing complexity, making it hard to predict exact memory usage, and risk of inconsistencies.

7.6. Resource Utilization

When it comes to resource use, STW algorithms engross all available processing power for the garbage collection process. However, persistent throughout the lifetime of the application, Concurrent GCs usually require more CPU resources, which might affect the overall performance of the app.

7.7. Synchronization Overhead

In stopping the application altogether during garbage collection, STW algorithms circumvent the issues of synchronization overhead. Conversely, concurrent GCs should deal with locks and atomic operations to prevent any undesirable race conditions from occurring. It ratchets up the overhead due to continual checks and balances to prevent inconsistency.

7.8. Reinforcing Responsiveness

Here, the Concurrent GC takes the crown. By working in parallel with the application, it supports responsiveness. The system doesn't stop, implying limited visible interruption to the user, making it a valuable option for interactive applications.

Taking these parameters into account pulls back the veil on the multifaceted nature of garbage collection algorithms. It's notable that there is no definite answer to the question of supremacy between STW and Concurrent. The appropriate method depends on the requisites, constraints, and nature of the system at hand. By understanding the intricacies of 'Stop-The-World' and 'Concurrent' garbage collection, one can fine-tune their systems to establish the synergy between user demands and computer capabilities, therefore optimizing the potential of computational systems.

Chapter 8. Optimization Techniques in Garbage Collection

Living in the intricate dance of machine logic, the Garbage Collection (GC) Algorithms breathe life into antiquated systems and make them resilient, agile and optimized. These invisible maestros of memory management might seem daunting but adopt an elegant simplicity when viewed through the lens of their underlying optimization techniques, allowing them to make quick and critical decisions regarding the memory lifecycle.

8.1. Memory Management: The Core of Garbage Collection

The crux of any garbage collection algorithm lies in its mastery over memory management. A successful garbage collector knows when to allocate or deallocate memory in sync with the ebb and flow of computational processes. As part of the allocation process, memory is assigned to objects when they're created, gifting them with a space to exist and function within the system. However, this memory space isn't endless, leading to the requirement to recycle memory that's no longer serving a purpose.

Deallocation kicks in when objects fall out of use — when they're not reachable in the code, or when they're explicitly deleted. Herein lies the core challenge in garbage collection: recognizing the precise moment when objects are no longer in use.

8.2. Mark and Sweep: The Fundamental Framework

The Mark and Sweep technique is instrumental in understanding the mechanics of Garbage Collection. It consists of two distinct phases: 'Mark' and 'Sweep'.

Mark Phase: During this phase, the algorithm dives into a deep search, starting from a root object and marking all reachable objects. Marking is akin to keeping a note of important data which should continue to occupy memory space.

Sweep Phase: As the name suggests, this phase sweeps through the memory heap and clears out objects that haven't been marked, effectively freeing up memory. This phase generally triggers once the 'Mark' phase concludes.

The ingenuity in this framework lies in its ability to defragment the memory heap. Consequently, its prowess allows for memory to be used more effectively in subsequent allocation requests.

8.3. Generational Garbage Collection: Harnessing the Power of Heuristics

The Generational GC leverages a powerful hypothesis known as the 'Generational Hypothesis', asserting that most objects die young. Therefore, more recent objects have a higher probability of becoming garbage sooner.

This technique segments memory into different generations — usually two: 'Young' and 'Old'. Objects that survive collection in the 'Young' space (New Generation) over a period of time are promoted to the 'Old' space (Survivor Generation), forming the foundation of a two-step garbage collection.

Minor GC: This process performs collection in the 'Young' generation only. It's faster than collecting from the 'Old' generation due to a smaller space to traverse and is performed more frequently due to the generational hypothesis.

Major GC: Involves collecting from the 'Old' generation which incurs higher costs due to the larger coverage area. It's known to cause a 'stop-the-world' event wherein all application threads are halted.

Learning to balance minor and major garbage collection consequently becomes the secret sauce of system optimization.

8.4. Concurrent and Parallel Garbage Collection: Minimizing Pauses

Concurrent GC operates simultaneously with the application whereas Parallel GC uses multiple threads during the 'Mark' and 'Sweep' phase. The former can reduce pauses, during which an application can appear unresponsive, while the latter can speed up garbage collection overall in multi-core environments.

However, these come with trade-offs. Concurrent GC might decrease pause times but increases overhead as collection and application operations jostle for CPU time. Parallel GC, on the other hand, might speed up the collection process but can lead to decreased application throughput if the increased GC threads compete with application threads for resources.

8.5. Magic of Incremental and Compacting GC techniques

The Incremental GC breaks down the 'Mark' and 'Sweep' phase into smaller units of work performed over intervals. This operation maintains a healthy balance between application run-time and GC pauses, establishing a steady rhythm of incremental system optimization.

Compacting GC directs its focus on combating memory fragmentation, an aftermath of the 'Sweep' phase of the Mark and Sweep technique. It moves live objects together, making allocation more efficient while also potentially improving cache performance by improving data locality.

In an era of demanding applications, understanding these optimizing techniques is fundamental to shaping an efficient system. Instead of treating garbage collection as a chore, appreciate the invisible elegance it provides. The mastery of these techniques propel applications into new dimensions of performance ensuring they remain dynamic, responsive, and efficient, playing their symphony in the orchestra of system design. This is the art ensuring longevity in the information age.

Chapter 9. Testing and Benchmarking Garbage Collection Algorithms

When talking about garbage collection algorithms, understanding their functioning is only half the task. Validating their effectiveness and efficiency comes down to judicious testing and benchmarking. This segment will thus guide you through this critical, yet often overlooked, aspect of garbage collection.

9.1. Conducting Proper Testing

Testing garbage collection algorithms requires an intricate, well-thought-out strategy. Simply running the algorithm and observing its surface output does not suffice. What's crucial is to dig deep and understand how it affects your system at various levels.

1. **Determining the Environment:** The first step is to decide the test environment. It should mimic your production environment as closely as possible. This may include considering factors like system configurations, volume of data, and the operation complexities. It should also include more specific parameters relevant to memory management, such as usage patterns, object life duration, available memory, and allocation rates.

2. **Identifying Key Parameters:** After setting up the test environment, you need to identify the crucial parameters to monitor and measure. These parameters indicate whether a garbage collector is functioning as expected, and they will primarily include memory usage, CPU usage, response time, and the number of garbage collection cycles per unit time.

3. **Choosing the Right Tools:** Once your key parameters are set, gather tools that can help you monitor and measure these

parameters while the test runs. Tools like the Java VisualVM, JProfiler, and NetBeans Profiler can be handy.

4. **Crafting the Test Case:** Create a test case as realistic as possible. It should include tasks and operations that actually appear in your applications. You may need to model situations where objects with different life spans are created at varying intervals.

5. **Executing and Monitoring:** After completing the preparations, run the test and keep a close watch on the identified parameters. Any irregularities or anomalies can indicate potential issues.

9.2. Benchmarking Garbage Collection Algorithms

On completing the tests, the next step is benchmarking the results. This essentially means comparing your results against those of other garbage collection algorithms, or potentially against previous versions of the same algorithm.

1. **Selecting a Baseline:** A component of achieving an effective benchmark is to determine an appropriate baseline. This could be a well-established, general-purpose garbage collector that has been proven to work efficiently in a variety of settings.

2. **Collecting Data:** One of the crucial steps in benchmarking is data collection. The data must be reliable, accurate, and relevant. While collecting data, it's crucial to ensure consistency in the environment and conditions for the test runs of different algorithms.

3. **Analyzing the Results:** Benchmarking is all about comparatives. Analyze each algorithm's outcome in detail in terms of the identified parameters. This could be average memory usage, CPU usage, or frequency of garbage collection cycles.

4. **Identifying Trade-offs:** In the world of algorithms, there's no one-size-fits-all. Engaging in benchmarking helps us better

understand the various trade-offs each algorithm presents. For instance, one algorithm might optimise for reduced memory usage at the cost of higher CPU usage.

9.3. The Role of Simulation in Testing and Benchmarking

Simulation plays a pivotal role in testing and benchmarking garbage collection algorithms. This is due to the inherent unpredictability and variability of garbage collection requirements in different applications. Simulation allows researchers and developers to model various scenarios and object lifespan distributions that might be encountered in real-world applications.

With the aid of accurate simulations, researchers can take the symbiotic relationship between the garbage collector and application to an unprecedented level of sophistication. After all, the primary goal of garbage collection algorithms is not just about cleaning up but also about efficiently managing resources to ensure optimal application performance. This goal can only be achieved when the algorithm is tested, benchmarked, and iteratively refined against a gamut of realistic scenarios in controlled environments.

To sum up, testing and benchmarking are integral to the development and refinement of effective and efficient garbage collection algorithms. These processes provide a framework to track the behavior of algorithms within the context of a desired specification or set of parameters, thereby facilitating improved understanding and optimisation. Remember, the fine-tuning ability one gains from meticulous testing could spell the difference between a mediocre application and an outstanding one.

Chapter 10. The Future of Garbage Collection: Predictions and Perspectives

Garbage Collection (GC), being an essential component of many computing systems, has seen significant progress in recent times. It has been continually optimized and restructured to cope with the increasing demand for effective memory management. Yet, speculating about the future can be as exciting as retracing the past. Technological advancements often spotlight emerging applications of GC and present new challenges that it must tackle smoothly. This chapter examines potential future developments in GC and presents some perspectives for how it may continue to evolve.

10.1. Advent of Quantum Computing

Quantum computing exploits quantum phenomena like superposition and entanglement to process information. What makes this quantum leap promising yet challenging is its distinctive memory architecture, which may require an evolution in garbage collection algorithms. The multi-state nature of quantum bits (also known as qubits) is expected to present unique GC demands not seen in classic computation.

Moreover, quantum error correction, a suite of algorithms responsible for maintaining the coherence of quantum information, will necessitate complex and efficient garbage collection mechanisms. They would need to handle the ephemeral 'quantum garbage' that gets created during these tasks and competes for valuable computing time. As more strides are made in this field, expect GC to adapt accordingly, leading to innovative solutions in quantum garbage handling.

10.2. Infusion of AI and Machine Learning

Artificial Intelligence (AI) and Machine Learning (ML) are revolutionizing almost every sphere of human activity, and GC is no exception to this. With the added cognitive capabilities of AI, GC could potentially predict memory usage patterns and manage resources more effectively. For instance, pre-emptive garbage collection could be initiatied during idle periods, ensuring constant high availability of system resources for critical tasks.

Working with ML, GC could learn from memory usage histories, adjusting its strategies depending on daily, weekly, or even yearly cycles. It could predict potential memory leaks before they become problematic, allowing software developers and system administrators to preemptively address these issues.

10.3. Bursting Cloud and Edge Computing

The advent of the Cloud and Edge Computing paradigms has brought with it an explosion of distributed systems spanning across several computing nodes. Such systems demand efficient memory management across disparate nodes and infrastructures. GC in this area will need to adeptly manage data deletion and movement across multiple tiers of storage, including volatile memory, non-volatile memory, SSDs, and network-based distributed storage.

Edge computing in particular presents new challenges, as smart devices with constrained resources need intelligent garbage collection strategies to keep up with real-time, high criticality tasks. Solutions could involve lightweight GC algorithms for constrained environments, alongside real-time garbage collection to ensure high system performance even under heavy load. Of particular interest is federated learning, where MLM models are trained across numerous decentralized devices. GC will play an important role in managing the local memory of devices without compromising performance and data privacy.

10.4. Growing Emphasis on Sustainability

Finally, the need for eco-friendly computing is pushing for trash-conscious hardware, software, and algorithms. GC can play a significant role here. Currently, GC operates largely oblivious to power consumption. However, future GC algorithms could employ power-efficient strategies.

Adaptive garbage collection that varies its strategy based on the system's idle and busy periods could save energy. In addition, by combining power-efficient GC algorithms with 'green' hardware optimized for low power consumption, we could achieve truly sustainable computing.

10.5. Conclusion

The future of GC appears to be as colorful as its past. From quantum computing where it will dance with qubits, to AI and ML where it will gracefully outsmart memory challenges, GC will continue to evolve. It will help distribute systems to function efficiently and facilitate 'green' computing. As we continue our journey into the Information Age, we can rest assured knowing that GC, our silent digital sentinel, is always at work, optimizing performance for each leap into the future.

Chapter 11. Case Studies: Real-world Applications of Garbage Collection Algorithms

Garbage Collection, heavily upheld for its impact on memory management, has found its implementation in real-world scenarios ranging from the microscopic segment of app development, all the way up to large-scale system optimization. This chapter embarks on an exploration of both classical and contemporary case studies, encapsulating applications across brewing industries like tech, finance, academia, and beyond.

11.1. Application in Java

Fundamental to its legacy, the application of Garbage Collection algorithms in Java remains an illuminating case study. Java is a high-level, object-oriented programming language, designed specifically to be as dependably enduring as possible. The automatic memory management, or 'Garbage Collection', plays a significant role in lending to Java's long-lasting usability.

Within Java, Garbage Collection algorithms work by segregating memory into distinct parts, namely the "Eden Space" where all new objects get created, and two "Survivor Spaces" where long-lasting objects transit through. This process, as a part of the 'New Generation', contrasts with the 'Old Generation' which houses stable, long-term data, delivering a well-structured system of memory management ensuring effective application performance.

11.2. Server Optimization with Garbage Collection

Beyond programming languages, Garbage Collection algorithms find prime utility in server systems, dovetailing efficiency and performance with the manner in which memory resources are allocated. Servers stand as intricate mechanisms, yet are often susceptible to issues of system slowdown and latency. Major contributing factors include incorrect configuration of GC threads and wrong settings of GC modes, causing issues like frequent, long-term pauses.

Monolithic servers or micro-services, regardless of scale, profit significantly from wisely configured mirroring between GC and server loads, ensuring efficient resource handling, lower latency, and steady performance. For instance, Twitter famously modified their GC approach from CMS (Concurrent Mark Sweep) to G1GC (Garbage First Garbage Collector) to reduce the plethora of smaller, frequent pauses resulting from former GC algorithm.

11.3. Parallel, Concurrent, and Real-Time Garbage Collection in Operating Systems

The realm of operating systems, a critical territory of computation, exhibits potential for Garbage Collection application, principally via the integration of parallel, concurrent, and real-time GC.

Parallel GC incorporates simultaneous execution across multiple cores, exhibiting effective for multi-processor systems and highly threaded applications. Concurrent GC, on the other hand, seeks to reduce pause time by collecting garbage concurrently with the application thread. This proves fruitful where response time is critical. Real-Time GC ensures that GC is executed within specific deadlines, beneficial in real-time systems where timing of operation's execution is crucial.

11.4. Role in Enhancing Microservice Architecture

Microservices, the architectural style that structures an application as a collection of services, derive significant benefit from Garbage Collection algorithms. Microservices employ discrete processing units, implying potential resource waste if memory isn't carefully managed across numerous individually operating units.

Utilizing GC algorithms in this setting ensures optimum efficiency, especially with the apt choice of GC algorithm responsive to the type, scale, and objectives of the specific workloads at hand. GC's ability to clean out unneeded, stale data to free up memory resources, in the context of independently executing services, proves crucially beneficial.

11.5. Concluding Remarks

Garbage Collection algorithms don't get to enjoy marquee lighting often, yet they are silently hard at work, shaping tomorrow's efficient, performant, and scalable systems. They are coded emperors of the digital kingdom, and their expansion beyond classic computer science into every corner of the tech world bears testimony to their vital role in the digital age.

Whether part of Java's celebrated memory management system or bolstering server performance, whether negotiating constraints of operating systems or maximizing efficiency in the realm of Microservices, the reign of Garbage Collection algorithms echoes across the technological expanse. It is an invisible fabric interwoven intrinsically within the digital landscape, a testament to the unparalleled efficacy of efficient memory management in shaping contemporary computational paradigms.

www.ingramcontent.com/pod-product-compliance
Lightning Source LLC
LaVergne TN
LVHW051629050326
832903LV00033B/4709